My Furry, Four-Footed Friends

Footed Friends

And Other Creatures Great and Small

DJ Clancy

authorHOUSE®

AuthorHouse™
1663 Liberty Drive
Bloomington, IN 47403
www.authorhouse.com
Phone: 1 (800) 839-8640

Published by AuthorHouse 12/05/2016

ISBN: 978-1-5049-5762-5 (sc)
ISBN: 978-1-5049-7817-0 (e)

Library of Congress Control Number: 2016920016

Print information available on the last page.

Any people depicted in stock imagery provided by Thinkstock are models, and such images are being used for illustrative purposes only.
Certain stock imagery © Thinkstock.

This book is printed on acid-free paper.

Contents

Acknowledgements

To my family and friends for their continued support and encouragement. It has been quite a ride. My love always.

To my husband Gary for putting up with all my animals and crazy antics through the years. Without your acceptance of my critters, I would not have had any material. Love and hugs!

To Tony Borek for retrieving my manuscript when I thought it was lost forever on my aging laptop. Thank you, thank you.

To Sam McCabe of Sage Consulting for your ideas, honest advice and encouragement in organizing a great website. Your talent is amazing and your input is much appreciated.

To Ann Wirtz, of Wirtz Design Studio's for organizing my pictures again for this book.

www.djclancy.com

www.facebook.com/DJClancyAuthor

Introduction

Friends? Yes, my animals are my friends. Sometimes they are there for me more than humans are. I know I'll get flak for this, but think about it. There are different kinds of love. Love between a husband and a wife. Love for your children and love between siblings. Love for your parents, love between friends, deep love and deep friendships. The kind of love that grows with time. You would do anything in your power for the people you love, right? And they would do anything for you. Love never goes away, but children grow up and leave the nest to make their own lives, as they should.

My husband Gary, myself and our two children moved around the country to start our own lives thus leaving our families in New York. We see them often and the family reunions are always special. We also have many wonderful friends. Some live close and others far away, so time spent together is always special. But when I reflect on who has been here for me 24/7, it's my animals. They are never in a bad mood or too busy for me. They are always happy to see me, no matter how long I may have been away. All they want to do is be with me, even if I'm in a bad mood, sad, or in a hurry.

My husband, Gary, once heard the following joke: If you locked your dog and your wife in the trunk of your car, which one would be happy to see you when you opened it up? I'll bet you know the answer.

This book is for those of you who have experienced the love of an animal, whether it was a dog, cat, horse, or even a hamster. In this book, I reflect on how different—and similar—dogs and cats are, and how they have different means of achieving the same goals. The first chapters of this book come from my mother's memory, and the later sections are drawn from my own. Included here are stories of my cats' and my dogs' behaviors, and stories about a few other critters I've met along the way. Of course, every animal is different, just as we humans are all different. And if we are really fortunate, we discover a love between us and an animal that is a once-in-a-lifetime experience. That love can be so deep that it continues even after the death of that animal. A soul mate, maybe? I'll let you be the judge of that.

Dogs versus Cats

People will tell you dogs and cats are as different as day and night. Of course, they do look and act differently, but maybe they are similar, too. Maybe they want some of the same things, but they go about getting those things in different ways.

Dogs can be stubborn, especially as puppies and during training sessions, but they will eventually obey you because they want to please you. Cats, on the other hand, want you to please them. They come to you when they are good and ready. They want to eat at a certain time, and they won't touch food that was their favorite the previous week. I would open can after can of cat food, until our cats would decide which kind they liked that day. And then their attitude was "Don't even try to give me the can of food from yesterday." Now, as I said earlier, there are exceptions to all behaviors. I can only speak of my critters.

I had several cat beds and blankets around the house for my two cats, Dixon and Lexie, because my little cuties liked a variety. One week they would sleep on the bed in my office. The next week they preferred my bedroom, or they would curl up on the sofa without a blanket. One day they slept on a new dress that I wanted to wear that night, after kneading it with their claws until their little nest felt just right.

My cats also had this amazing ability to know which of my friends didn't like cats, and it was their mission to jump on those people every chance they had. Even if the cats got pushed off someone's lap, it didn't matter. They would go right back to the people who didn't like them. Dixon had black hair and Lexie was a light gray, so Dixon would jump up on the laps of people who wore white, and Lexie would take the people who wore black. They didn't care if the people were male or female—either way, Dixon and Lexie were out to get them. I kept a collection of lint brushes by the front door to give to our guests as party favors when they went home.

In contrast, Barnaby, my dog, would curl up on his one bed in our bedroom every night. At least he started in his bed. But sometimes, in the dead of night, he would creep up onto the foot of our bed.

You are probably wondering why I love animals so much and write books about them. Let me share my backstory with you. It all started on a farm...

In My Mother's Memory

My love for animals comes from my parents, especially my mom. When I was growing up, we always had at least one cat. My mom is from a small town in northern Germany, and my dad from a small town in Austria.

When he was eighteen, my father enlisted in the air force. He was promised that after two years of service, the air force would help him get a job on the outside. Then came World War II and he was sent to the Russian front, with promises of leaving the service after two years forgotten. He drove artillery trucks for seven years, before being shot through the wrist near the end of the war. A buddy dragged my father to a field medic tent where doctors wanted to amputate his hand. Field hospitals were understaffed and undersupplied, much like on the TV show *M.A.S.H.*, and the doctors were just trying to save as many lives as they could. My father's buddy pleaded with the doctor to save Dad's hand because he played the violin. So the doctor patched my father's wrist the best he could, wished him good luck, and shipped him off to a real hospital in northern Germany. There Dad met my mother, who volunteered at the hospital as an aide.

My parents married a year later, in April 1948. Even though the war was over, there was still a shortage of food. Mom had a friend whose parents owned a farm, so she asked for one egg and some milk for a wedding cake. My grandmother, who had just received a package from America containing coffee, traded the coffee to her local butcher in return for a beef roast, which was my parents' wedding dinner. The church in town had been bombed, so the minister came to their apartment to perform the ceremony. Mom's dress was her confirmation dress and Dad got a suit from the Salvation Army.

I was born a year later, and we were able to move to my great-grandparents' house, a small farmhouse seventy-five miles south of the Danish border in a place called Schleswig. Since our house was in the country, there weren't many neighborhood children with whom to play, so animals became my friends. I would play with them and dress up the cats in baby clothes. My mother often found a stray animal that was hungry or needed tending. A baby porcupine who started coming around the farm become a family pet. It would go on its travels during the day and return to our house for food at night. Mom would put him in my lap, where he stayed, never hurting me with his quills.

After several months on the farm, we adopted a wild bird named Jacob. My uncle, Mom's younger brother, was only seven years older than me, and he too found creatures that needed his help. Finding a baby bird that had fallen out of its nest, my uncle took it home to nurse it back to health. Only this baby bird turned into a big bird, a raven, whom he named Jacob. My uncle and grandparents lived in Wilster, a small town about an hour south of us. They had an apartment over a bank and people didn't have screens for their windows, so Jacob came and went as he pleased, flying in and out of the apartment window. The only problem was that Jacob was a thief. He would come home at night with his treasures—sometimes a little doll from a dollhouse, one time a small plastic bracelet, and more times than not, clothespins. Back then, people used clothespins to hold their freshly laundered clothes on a line to dry. Jacob would fly by and pluck the pins off the line, causing the clothes to fall on the ground. The women would yell and chase the bird away with their brooms, but that raven always returned to my grandparents' apartment when it got dark and sat on a perch my uncle had made for him.

My grandmother was always cleaning up after Jacob, especially after he would groom himself and pluck his feathers. She could have made a pillow with all the feathers she swept up. One afternoon my grandmother decided to bake a cake. That was unusual, because scarce ingredients such as eggs, flour, and butter were used to make meals, not to bake a cake. Jacob, who had been out getting into trouble as usual, suddenly flew into the kitchen. He flew a little too low, however, and his wing dipped into my grandmother's cake batter. Needless to say, she screamed at the bird and at my uncle, "Out! That bird has to go!"

That's how my parents and I came to adopt Jacob. Dad made a perch for him on our front porch, and he flew in and out of our house just as he had my grandparents' apartment. That raven came to love my mom. When she went to the market, he would wait high in a tree until he saw her coming down the road riding her bicycle. Then he would swoop down and escort her home while sitting on the bicycle's handlebars. Jacob also would share breakfast with my dad, dipping his beak in Dad's coffee and eating crumbs of toast as they both got ready for their day.

Living in the country, with lots of farms around, meant more mischief for Jacob to get into. He would tease chickens by swooping down to get some of their food. Then, just in the nick of time, he would fly back up and out of their way. That would cause such a commotion that the farmer would come out with his pitchfork to see what the trouble was. By then, however, Jacob would be already high in a tree and laughing at all the fuss.

Jacob would sit on my shoulder in the garden or sometimes on my head while I played with our cat. A cat and a wild bird getting along just fine! Who would have thought? One afternoon, we heard our chickens in a frenzy in the chicken yard. When Mom went over to see what was going on, Jacob was there. That time, however, he didn't get away quickly enough, and the chickens got their revenge. Mom was in tears as she tried to save him, but it was too late. As she cried and talked to him, Jacob died in her arms. She wrapped him in a soft blanket, and we buried him under the apple tree where he used to sit and wait for Mom.

We visited my dad's parents in Austria before coming to America. They had lots of farm animals, including goats rather than cows. Every morning the families in the village would open their barn doors, the goats would gather in the square, and the goat herder would take the goats high up the mountain for fresh green grass. Then he would return the herd of goats to the town square at night— and each goat would find the way home to its own barn, where it was time for milking. Mom said I didn't like goats' milk, but that was all we had. So it was goats' milk for all. Maybe my love of animals really came from drinking goats' milk for two weeks in the mountains of Austria.

Coming to America

How brave my father was to take his young family so far away, to a strange land, not knowing what the future held. Was it the right decision? Would he find a job to provide for us? He'd been told that America was the land of opportunity, and he prayed it was true.

We sailed for twelve days on a ship called the *Neptunia*, a luxury liner. When the war had broken out, she had been used to transport troops. After the war, she was used to transport immigrants to a new world and a new life. I don't remember much of the journey, since I was just shy of four years old, although I do remember being very sad to leave Grandmother and my uncle. Maybe, after all these years, my brain is so full that I've deleted some earlier memories, but then, I might just be getting older.

As we sailed past the Statue of Liberty, Dad held us tightly, hoping he had made the right decision to bring his family to this new world. As we disembarked, with everything we owned in our three suitcases, our aunt and uncle were at the dock to take us to our new home. They had a chicken farm on eastern Long Island, with a small bungalow behind the main house for us.

Mom worked on the farm candling eggs the old-fashioned way, by a light in a black box with a small hole in it. She held the egg up to the light to see whether it was fertilized. If it was clean, it was put in an egg carton for my uncle to deliver to customers. He would drive every morning at five thirty to deliver the eggs and milk, and sometimes I was allowed to go with him.

Being a girly girl, I loved to play dress up and put on old petticoats and dresses that had belonged to my cousin, who lived in the main house. Uncle would say I could come with him on his morning delivery route, but that I'd have to leave the petticoat behind. "No," I said, and after that I never went with him again. I guess I embarrassed him with my dressing up. My stubbornness must have started back then. I was four years old, after all, and a woman with a mind of my own. And once again, I was living on a farm where there weren't many children around until I started kindergarten, so the farm animals became my friends.

Dad took any job he could find. He then taught himself to be a mechanic on Volkswagens, working his way up to service manager for Volkswagen Worldwide.

Growing up on the farm, I had a tame parakeet named Charlie who loved my dad's coffee and flew around the house as he pleased, a baby water turtle that I found in a nearby river, and, of course, cats. We also had several dogs through the years, as well as the farm animals—chickens, cows, and cattle. I befriended a cute little heifer with little white curls on top of his head. He came to me often to give him some hay, and I called him Curley.

One Sunday, my aunt had prepared a wonderful, farm-fresh dinner with all the trimmings. As we were enjoying the meal, I asked my uncle where Curley was, since I hadn't seen him in a few days. My uncle looked at me, laughed, and said, "You're eating him." Well, I got up from the table, ran outside, and violently threw up. *How could he?* I wondered. Mom followed me and tried to explain that on a farm, animals are raised as food. But I couldn't get over Curley's death, and it stayed with me for years. When I was older, I could understand, but I'll never forget the way my uncle told me.

We became proud citizens of the United States of America five years later, and bought a car and house. Our family vacations were spent in the Catskill or Adirondack Mountains in upstate New York. One year we came upon a reptile farm deep in the forests of the Adirondacks. Since they had every type of reptile you could think of, we decided to go in and take a look. A staff member was giving a lecture on snakes, and as we listened, he gave one to me to hold—a pretty yellow snake about two feet long. I have to admit that as I held that creature, I really didn't feel the love. I know that lots of people love snakes, but I prefer creatures with fur.

As a matter of fact, I really don't care for spiders, fleas, or ticks either. When I go before those pearly gates, I will ask Him the purpose of the flea. My husband Gary says fleas are here to give animals exercise. We scratch when they bite us, and I guess that qualifies as exercise. When a dog or a cat gets a flea bite, they scratch, too. Imagine being in a spinning class and pedaling with only one leg at a time, and then think about what dogs and cats look like when they're scratching. See the similarity?

After I ask about fleas, I'm going to ask Him what happened to all those socks that went into the washing machine but never came out. And then I'll ask about all those keys that I lost over the years. I already know where old running shoes go. There is a tree on the side of the road in St. George, Utah, that is full of old shoes. There must be hundreds of them hanging in that tree. No leaves, just old running shoes, so Gary, being a runner, left a contribution to that tree as well.

On the Move

Gary worked for a large corporation, and was transferred to Syracuse, New York, shortly after our son Sean was born. As we were driving to our new apartment, we noticed six-foot poles next to every fire hydrant. Wonder what that's all about? Well, we found out during our first winter. Our first snowstorm in Syracuse was so intense that all the cars in the parking lot were covered in six-to seven-foot drifts. Aha! Then we understood the poles! They were placed next to fire hydrants so the fire department could find them in the snow. Now, that made sense. Children were sledding down roofs and across cars into snow, snow, and more snow.

I found a little kitty that hung around the apartment complex and would just sit with me when the children played outside. I never did find out where she belonged, but I figured she had a home since she never seemed hungry. Oh, I wanted a cat so badly, but pets were not allowed in the apartments.

Not only did we have severe winters, but we also had snow from Halloween until Easter. Our daughter Nicole was born the next year, so our children were only twenty months apart in age. It was always a challenge to dress Sean and Nicole to play in the snow, because they wore one-piece snowsuits. Sometimes I would get Sean all dressed with boots and gloves in his suit. But as I started to dress Nicole, Sean had to go to the bathroom. Everything had to come off because his snowsuit was one piece. By then Nicole was hot, plus she had begun undressing because she, too, had to go to the bathroom. Oh, the power of suggestion. By then I was exhausted, but round and round we went.

Finally, with Sean and Nicole looking like Pillsbury Doughboys, all three of us were ready to brave the cold. But a mere fifteen minutes later, we were frozen popsicles and retreated to our warm apartment to cozy up and watch cartoons. It took us more than half an hour to get dressed for fifteen minutes of fun in the snow. Go figure.

After two years of snow, Gary's employer transferred him to Dallas, Texas, where we bought our first house and adopted Casey, our first cat. I was so happy to have a cat in my life again. *This is perfect*, I thought. We lived in Bedford, a rural area between Dallas and Fort Worth. It was a new development surrounded by lots of open fields. Most of the families were young, just like us, so we all became good friends.

One evening at dusk, Gary and I were in our front yard talking with some neighbors while our children were playing in the street. Suddenly, by the glow of the streetlight, we saw a family of skunks—a mama and four little ones—come out of the field. Gary said, "Nobody move!" We held our breath as the little family walked into our garage. We just stood there, hoping they wouldn't get scared, because everyone knows what happens when a skunk feels threatened. A few minutes later, they waddled out of our garage and back into the field without leaving a distinctive perfume, if you know what I mean. Whew!

Two years later, Gary was transferred to Pleasanton, California, and we decided it would be fun to drive across the country with the kids. What did we do about Casey? Well, we had a great neighbor who kept him until we were in California and then shipped him to us by plane. Being an animal lover, she wanted to make sure Casey had a good trip, so she fed him a nice big breakfast before sending him on his way. When I went to the San Francisco airport cargo area to pick him up, the attendant laughed and gave me a very strange look. When he brought Casey out, I understood. Even before I saw my cat, I could smell him. Poor Casey had thrown up and pooped all over the cage, and you can just imagine what he looked like. Now what? It was a long drive home, so I opened all the car windows and hung *my* head out.

Unfortunately, the worst was still to come. Casey needed a bath—but Casey *hated* baths, so I had to protect myself. I put Casey in the backyard in his cage. *Sorry, guy, just a few more minutes while I put on my armor.* Bathtub full of water? Check. Pet shampoo available and close at hand? Check. Bathroom window open? Check. Room deodorizer? Check. But the very most important things were my protective apron and long, heavy, latex gloves. Then I was ready for battle—and what a battle it was. Casey was not a happy kitty.

How much mess can a little kitty make? Let me count the ways. Poop and lather smeared all over the walls, the bathroom floor, and me. Gallons of excess water on the floor tiles as I struggled to maintain my balance. And then there were the cat sounds. I didn't know cats could make that many different noises.

By the end of Casey's bath, I was as wet as him and needed a bath myself! But I had managed to protect all the skin on my arms, and I wasn't going to need any plastic surgery on my face. Casey ran under our bed, where he stayed until dinnertime. When he finally emerged, he looked at me as if to say, "Don't ever do that again!" Well, have no fear. It wasn't pleasant for me, either, my furry friend.

Our stay in Pleasanton was short, because Gary's company soon transferred him to Basking Ridge, New Jersey, where the kids started school. Casey adjusted to his new home, but he never adjusted to the snow. He was a warm-weather cat from Texas and California, and the cold, white stuff on the ground was not to his liking at all! When winter came, Casey became an indoor cat and thus required a litter box. It was a messy job, but somebody had to do it—which meant me. We adopted a hamster, which Casey thought was his new toy. His eyes got wide while his tail swatted back and forth, as if he had just been given the best filet mignon in the world!

Our little hamster was an escape artist who frequently got out of his cage. I'd find him under the bed, in my daughter's closet, or in one of her shoes. When the hamster escaped, our first question was always, "Where's Casey?" Had he already found the hamster? Casey did manage to corner the hamster a few times and bat him around, but he never ate him, thank goodness. One cold winter day the hamster escaped again, and I couldn't find him for a long time. It turned out that he had managed to make his way down the hall and into my closet, but he wasn't moving. At first I thought Casey had finally had too much fun with him, but there were no marks on the little hamster. He was just very cold and stiff. I cried as I put him next to my heart on my bare skin to warm him, fearing the worst. I covered him with a warm blanket over my chest and tried to think how best to tell my daughter when she got home from school. After a few minutes, however, I felt a scratching on my chest. That little hamster was moving. He was still alive! I couldn't believe it. He lived a couple more years, as did Casey. But that same weekend, we purchased a new cage that successfully thwarted his subsequent escape attempts.

In 1984, we moved to Santa Barbara, California, where we rented a house from someone who didn't allow animals. But I just couldn't resist a cute little black kitten I saw in a pet shop, so I brought him home and we named him Timothy. Since the rental house was for sale, the real estate agent occasionally brought prospective buyers over to view it. She called one day saying she'd be over in half an hour.

But where could I hide Timothy? In fact, where *was* Timothy? He was too young to go outside, so he had to be in the house somewhere. Too late! The doorbell rang and in came the entourage. I held my breath as they went from room to room, waiting to hear, "You can't have that cat here." But the real estate agent didn't say a word. When they came back to the living room, there was Timothy on the back of the sofa, just lying there and looking around at everyone. I positioned myself between my cat and the real estate agent, hoping to block her view of my cat—and hoping we weren't about to hear a soft little "Meow." As they were leaving through the front door, Timothy jumped off the couch just in time to see them as I closed the door. They never knew.

The house sold, so we had to move. Just before the move, Timothy didn't come home one night. I called and called him, but he never came back. We had a large field behind our house, so we think it was coyotes. I was so sad, thinking of his last moments. Sometimes the ways of nature are hard to accept.

We met a wonderful golden retriever that came over every day when the kids got home from school. We didn't know his name or where he belonged; he just came by to play with the kids. We named him Marmaduke. That was our introduction to golden retrievers, and we fell in love with this gentle breed. One day as Marmaduke was leaving, I tied a note to his collar asking where he lived and explaining that he visited us often. I put our phone number on the note, and sure enough, that night a woman called. She had been wondering where he went every afternoon. She lived right down the street, and we became fast friends as well as tennis partners.

Settling into our new home, I needed some animals. We adopted a cat whom we named Dixon, and then another one named Toby. But Toby developed cancer early in his life, so we had to make the sad decision to let him go.

A year later, along came Lexie, a long-haired gray kitty. Then we also found our first dog, a golden retriever whom we named Barnaby. I didn't know much about dogs, so it took us a while to learn all the doggie do's and don'ts. I realized that Barnaby and our cats were different, of course, but they also shared some similarities in how they achieved their goals.

The cats would sit for hours over a mole mound, waiting for that little critter to pop its head out of the ground, or watching for a lizard to emerge out of the crevasse in a rock. When they caught that elusive lizard, they would bring it inside as a present for me. But first they'd play with it, which usually meant biting off its tail or just plain killing it. If finding a lizard's tail was as lucky as finding a cat's whisker, I'd be a lucky camper. One day I walked upstairs and found a large lizard staring at me from the top step—and Dixon sitting at the bedroom door. All three of us froze. What should I do? I sure wasn't going to catch a lizard with my bare hands. What if he ran under my bed or, even worse, jumped on top of it? Slowly I backed down the stairs, grabbed a towel, tiptoed back up the stairs, threw the towel over the lizard, and pounced on it. Yes, I pounced. I didn't want that creature to slither out. Dixon gave a yowl, as if to say, "I was still playing with him." But I managed to contain the lizard in the towel and let him out in our front yard to live another day.

Barnaby, on the other hand, would find that mole mound, look at it for all of five seconds, and then start digging. He'd follow that mole's scent all around the yard until he was finally exhausted, and with no mole to show for his troubles. But our yard ended up with trenches deep enough to install a new sprinkler system.

Two years old with my cat in Germany

Mom, me and Jacob

Arriving in America-April 12, 1953

Charlie and me

Some of my critters

Dad's shepherd

The long yellow snake

Puppy Brady

Brady with the bank's teddy bear

Big Sam

Breakfast with Opa

Samantha and Brady sharing my couch

Merry Christmas

Big dog parade with the therapy dog group

Brooklyn

Sweet Kitty-Kitty

Oh what a ride we had!

Teeth Versus Nails

Big dogs have big teeth that can do a lot of damage. Cats have small teeth, but big fangs. Did you know there are more germs in a cat's mouth than in a dog's? We found out in a way that could have been deadly.

My mom and dad had a cat named Sam. As he grew older, Sam became aggressive with Mom, attacking her ankles as she walked by or scratching her arm for no reason. One day he bit my dad on the forearm. Mom cleaned up the blood, but the puncture wound was still visible. Two days later Dad's arm turned red, and by day three a red line had started to go up his arm. Mom took him to the hospital emergency room, since apparently the infection in his arm had turned into blood poisoning. The poison was traveling up his arm to his heart, and if that had happened, he could have died. While Dad was being admitted, his temperature skyrocketed, so he was placed on strong antibiotics immediately. Nothing was working. I flew home to New York as soon as I heard he was in the hospital. More antibiotics were administered, but the fever didn't break. After day six, he finally started to improve. He was in the hospital for ten days because of that cat. How terribly sad it would have been to lose Dad because of a cat bite.

One morning I was in a tremendous amount of pain on one shoulder, so I went to my doctor. When the doctor examined me, he let out a gasp. On my upper arm, shoulder, neck, and down my back were deep, bloody scratches with red, oozing welts.

My doctor said, "My God, you've been attacked. We have to report this to the police immediately."

"Hold on, Doc. I know the perp. My cat Lexie did the dastardly deed." The doctor was shocked that a cat could do that much damage, so I proceeded to explain.

Early on the previous morning, I had been holding Lexie like a baby over my shoulder, snuggling with her as I went out the kitchen door to the backyard. At that exact moment, my neighbor put something in his trash can, right on the other side of the hedge, and the lid slammed shut. That noise scared Lexie, who used me as a launch pad to jump as far away from the noise as she could. It was a warm summer morning, so I had been wearing a tank top. Not much protection there. My doctor put me on strong antibiotics for ten days and pain medication for several days. After that, I always remembered to treat a cat like a cat, not a baby.

Cats have come and gone throughout my life, and it is always sad to have to say goodbye. After we lost Dixon, I came across a skinny little kitten in a pet shop. She was dark gray with big ears, four white paws, a white belly, and a milk mustache. She looked like the poster cat for the famous "Got milk?" campaign. It was 6:00 p.m., the store was closing, and I had to get home to start dinner. I thought about that little kitty all night, and at nine o'clock the next morning I was at the pet shop ready to bring her home. I wasn't sure how Lexie would react, but I just had to bring the skinny kitten, whom I named Samantha, into our family. We listened to lots of hissing and spitting for a few days, but then Lexie accepted that little one. They became good friends, eventually sleeping together on the couch.

Me and the Gorilla

Odd title for a chapter, you might think.

Gary's fiftieth birthday was approaching and I wanted it to be memorable, so I planned a surprise birthday party. But what else could I do so he would always remember it? I had read about a company where you can hire a person to come dressed as a clown, a butler, or a variety of other characters for a party. When I called, the owner listed all the costumes, but then she specifically mentioned a female gorilla suit. *How perfect*, I thought. Hired!

The day before the party, the owner called to tell me that the girl who was scheduled to come to my house was sick and they didn't have a substitute. But I could have the suit for free and find someone to play the part. A lightbulb went off: me! I was silly enough to pull it off, and it would be even better than a stranger, so I picked up the suit and informed my daughter, Nicole, of the plot.

When the house was full of friends and laughter, Nicole and I snuck out the back door to the side of the house, where I dressed in the gorilla suit. It was a furry black suit with a huge gorilla head topped with a pink bow. I enhanced the outfit with black gloves, black stiletto heels, and a handful of balloons. Then I went around to the front door and rang the bell. Show time!

When Gary opened the front door and saw a girl gorilla, he turned to run back into the house. I pursued him, blowing kisses and flirting with a seductive swagger. Someone yelled, "She's going to strip!" I didn't want anyone to figure out that it was me in the gorilla suit, so as soon as I cornered Gary, I rubbed up against him. The poor guy was really sweating it. Then off came the gorilla head and the crowd went wild! They couldn't believe it was me. Laughter erupted with howls and "You had us all." It certainly was a birthday Gary would never forget. For weeks afterward, our friends would drop off gorilla cards or stuffed gorillas with notes that said, "Well done."

Hence this chapter title, "Me and the Gorilla."

Why This Puppy?

One day my neighbor called to tell me there was a litter of golden puppies up the street that I should see. It had been six years since we said had goodbye to Barnaby, and I just wasn't ready to love a dog again. But my neighbor persuaded me to go see the puppies. I fell in love with a little guy they called Tony, but—wouldn't you know?—he was promised to another family. I was heartbroken. I didn't really know that puppy, but for some reason I was devastated that we couldn't have him. Only later would I understand *why* I felt so strongly for that pup.

At nine o'clock that evening, after I had spent most of the day crying, Claudia, the puppies' owner, called to tell me she wanted us to have Tony. I was so happy that I started to cry again, but they were tears of incredible joy! When Claudia brought Tony to our house, with a little blue ribbon around his neck, my life changed forever.

My love for that puppy was so deep that it almost frightened me. What was it about that little guy? My husband, Gary, and I decided to rename him Brady O'Shea Clancy. Even as a puppy he had a kind of regal disposition about him, something special. Wherever we went, people were drawn to him. Everyone wanted to meet him and hug him. We did the usual puppy training and all but he was always drawn to people more than to other puppies. He played with other puppies, but it was as if he was older and wiser already—so he'd rather hang out with people.

We went to agility classes to practice off-leash training. Brady was pretty good at following my commands, although he wasn't very fast. One day in class I sent him into the tunnel and then ran to the other end to give him his next command, but he didn't come out. The tunnel moved as if he was stuck inside, but that couldn't be. What was going on in there? A minute later, Brady came prancing out with a stick in his mouth. He was a golden retriever, after all, so he had retrieved a stick. Where he got it, nobody knew. The trainer and I just looked at each other and laughed. Brady cocked his head to one side, and I swear I heard him say, "What's the problem? Aren't you proud of me? No one else found a stick." What? Did I hear my dog talk? Of course not. It must have been something I was thinking, right? Little did I know that that was just the beginning of our incredible journey together. Nevertheless, a career in agility was clearly out of the question.

Brady and I loved to go for walks in the neighborhood or along the beach. For him it was like reading the newspaper as he explored all the different smells from other dogs and other critters. He also went with us to restaurants and had the waiters eating out of his paw. Brady was a gentleman through and through. When we passed people, he would walk in front of them until they stopped to acknowledge him. Brady and I developed a once-in-a-lifetime bond. He always knew when I was going somewhere, and he would be waiting for me by the front door. Even when I changed my routine, he always seemed to sense what I was thinking. Brady went everywhere with me—to the bank, the store, church, schools, the hospital, and even a drive-through car wash. He was welcomed everywhere we went and always had a big smile on his face when someone bent down to pet him.

Then it clicked—Brady had been training me. That dog had chosen me to help him accomplish his purpose on this earth. He could read people and how they were feeling, and his purpose was to comfort them. When someone needed unconditional love, he went right up to them and leaned into them, as if to say, "It will be all right. I'm here now."

My daughter suggested that Brady become a therapy dog, and I realized that was what we were meant to do. What better way to comfort people than to go to hospitals or nursing homes where people are sad, stressed out, or sick? So we took the test for certification for Love on a Leash, a national therapy dog organization. We received our credentials and began visiting Cottage Hospital in Goleta. Brady was only one and a half years old, young for a therapy dog, but he was a natural. The patients and staff loved him. People would pet him, give him kisses and a cookie, and yes, even sing to him.

Gary and I were teaching a church youth group at the time, and we took the kids to a place called Hillside House, a home for people with cerebral palsy and special needs. Brady still had a lot of puppy in him and needed some discipline, but we took him with us anyway. As we walked down the hall of the facility, Brady was looking for food that might have been dropped. He wasn't really paying attention to much of anything else—or to me, for that matter. But when people came out of their rooms to meet Brady, they all wanted to pet him or hug him. The nurses gave him kisses and, yes, lipstick ended up on his forehead.

One nurse came over to tell me that they had a special patient named David, who hadn't spoken in three months. Perhaps Brady could be of comfort to him? The nurse put David's hand on Brady's fur as we all stood very still and watched. Then David leaned over in his wheelchair, put his arm around my dog, and said, "I love you, Brady." That was a moment I will never forget. Gary and I cried, as did the staff while David tried to smile. That's when Brady's calling was confirmed.

Move Over Darling

At bedtime, Samantha had a bed on my side, Lexi slept at my feet on top of the covers, and Brady had a big bed next to Gary's side. All was quiet on the western front as we settled in for the night. At two o'clock in the morning, however, I woke up feeling like a grilled cheese sandwich. I was all squished up and too warm, and someone was snoring into my ear.

I turned on the light to find Samantha curled up by my chest and Brady in the middle of the bed leaning against my back. They had climbed onto our bed after Gary and I had gone to sleep and made themselves quite comfortable. So comfortable, in fact, that Brady had all four legs stretched out and was taking up most of the bed. Samantha had been snoring, or was it Lexie? When I turned the light on, they all woke up and looked at me as if to say, "What's the problem?" Brady just stretched out more as Gary clung to the edge of the bed. "Really?" asked Gary. "What's wrong with this picture?"

That happened night after night, but one night Brady came up onto the bed a bit too early. I wasn't asleep yet, so I just listened while watching him by the light of the moon. He crawled up very slowly, put his front two paws on the bed, hesitated to make sure we were still asleep, and then gave a slight jump and got his back feet on the bed. He paused for a moment, then he very slowly moved between

Gary and me, he curled up into a ball, and then I heard the release of a breath as if he were saying, "Yes, I did it again!"

A couple of months later, it was time to get a new mattress. So what did we do? Being good parents, we went from queen-size to king-size to accommodate all creatures, human and animal. From then on, I had no more dreams of being a grilled cheese sandwich. As the years rolled on, all was quiet and peaceful except for occasional snoring from Samantha or Brady. Or was it Gary or me?

After our children went off to college, our home consisted of Gary, myself, Lexi, Samantha, and Brady. One morning at seven o'clock, I let the animals outside, as usual. Gary and I were busy with our day when I noticed I hadn't seen Lexie in some time. Brady and Samantha were in the backyard, but where was Lexie? It was 5:00 p.m., then 6:00 p.m. *Where are you, Lexie?* I called for her up and down our street, and Gary went over to the school to look for her. Then I joined him, thinking maybe she had been hit by a car and was injured. We looked under all the bushes and called for her, but nothing. I didn't sleep all night, still calling for her as I walked up and down our street in the dark.

The next morning, I found some of Lexie's fur in the gutter down near the creek. My heart sank as I realized what had happened to her. We had seen coyotes running down our street other mornings. One of them must have taken Lexie from our front lawn, because she had been an older cat who didn't wander anymore. We gathered all the tufts of fur we could find, put them in a little box, and buried Lexie in our backyard. I had nightmares about her final minutes for days. Samantha and Brady seemed to miss her, too. They had become very close, sleeping together in the foyer or a lounge chair.

Now that our children were out of the house, I had more time on my hands. I started to really notice Samantha and Brady in the backyard. Samantha would curl up under a plant, wait patiently until a hummingbird hovered over a flower, and then grab it. Sometimes she would kill the bird, but usually she brought it inside to show me and boast about her great feat. One time, she brought inside a live hummingbird, which then began flying around the living room. Samantha went crazy chasing the bird, I was chasing Samantha, and the poor hummingbird just wanted to escape. Samantha tried to jump up on our bookcase after that bird, but she fell and took several picture frames and candles with her. Finally, I opened the front door and the poor little hummingbird found its way outside. Freedom at last.

One day while I was sitting on the patio reading, I heard a rustling in the plants. Out came Samantha with a hummingbird in her mouth. With Brady by my side, I caught Samantha and patted her on the head to encourage her to let the bird go. She did let it go but as the little bird started to fly away, it flew right into Brady's open mouth! Brady had the funniest look on his face, probably because the bird was fluttering around in his mouth. When I said, "Drop it," he did, and the bird flew away. I couldn't believe it. What were the chances of that happening? That poor bird must have been traumatized for the rest of its little life. Samantha was looking at Brady, Brady was bewildered, and I was laughing out loud.

What Are You Thinking?

As I watch Samantha and Brady, I wonder what they are thinking when we talk to them. Do they understand us? So let's have a Q & A and ask them.

Question 1. Want to go for a ride?

Brady. I'm ready, I'm ready! When? Now? Hurry up. I'm already at the door. Hurry up!

Samantha. Are you crazy? But please, please, take the dog. Please?

Question 2. How about a bath?

Brady. Okay, if I have too. But only if I can play with the garden hose, spraying you while carrying it inside to play tug of war.

Samantha. How dare you suggest such a thing! I'm out of here. See you at dinner. Or maybe I'll make you look for me and worry.

Question 3. When you wag your tail, what do you really mean?

Brady. I am SOOOO happy to see you. I'll do anything you want. Need a slipper, a shoe, a paper?

Samantha. When I wag my tail, I'm really pissed off and an attack is imminent! I strongly suggest you do not piss me off!

Question 4. The word *come*.

Brady. Reporting, sir. What can I do for you? [Of course, Brady, I know you ignored this word for quite a while. But you finally got it.]

Samantha. Not in my vocabulary. Later, dude. I was just about to take a nap.

Question 5. The word *visitors*.

Brady. Yeah, someone else to pet me and love me. If I tilt my head, they'll give me a treat. I can be so cute!

Samantha. Let me see, who doesn't like cats? I'll get them so they never come back.

Question 6. The word *dinner*.

Brady. Yeah, of course I'm hungry. Always.

Samantha. Better not be leftovers, because that will piss me off—and you know what that means.

Question 7. The phrase *I'll be back.*

Brady. Please, please, don't leave me. I want to come.

Samantha. Whatever, Mom. Just leave quietly. I've got this lizard cornered.

Question 8. The word *beach*.

Brady. Oh yeah! Those wonderful smells, dead seals, snails, fish, and any scraps of food will do.

Samantha. Again, not in my vocabulary. And if it involves a car ride, forget it. But by all means, take the dog.

Question 9. The word *lizard*.

Brady. Let the chase begin!

Samantha. Now you're talking a great game. Peekaboo, I don't see you, but I'll wait until I do.

So there you have it. The inner thoughts of Samantha the cat and Brady the dog. What would your critters say?

Working the Room

After Brady was certified as a therapy pet, we regularly visited Goleta Valley Cottage Hospital. Brady wore a special badge and vest, and we went from room to room to visit patients and their families. He would snuggle his head on the lap of a patient, so that it looked like the two of them were having an intimate conversation. Sometimes patients would shed a tear into Brady's fur, and sometimes they whispered secrets that only Brady could hear and understand.

The patients came and went, but the staff stayed the same. Staff members loved Brady too, and they often gave him cookies, kisses, and hugs. We all became good friends and looked forward to our weekly visits. When Brady and I would arrive at the hospital, we always stopped at the nurses' station first to find out which patients were contagious or being treated for an infection or respiratory condition. Brady and I didn't go into their rooms, which protected all of us—the patient, me, and the dog.

One day a nurse said, "Don't go into room 104. The patient is elderly and very agitated. But worse, the son is very demanding, angry, and just plain mean."

"Okay," I said. Then Brady and I proceeded down the hall, but wouldn't you know it? He beelined it into room 104 before I could pull him back. *Well*, I thought, *there's no turning back now. Brady, work your magic.* As I entered the room, the son gave me a big smile. "Come in, come in," he said. The patient bent over from her bed to pet Brady, and all the tension left the room. They were head over heels in love with my dog, laughing and petting him, and Brady and I visited for quite a while.

When we came out of the room, the nurses were standing there and holding their breath. "You went in there? Are you two okay?" As Brady pranced toward them with a big grin on his face, I heard him say, "No problem. They loved me. I knew they would." That was the effect he had on everyone he encountered.

Another time at the hospital, we were on our way into the ICU when a family in the waiting room asked us to come in for a visit. There were about ten family members, nervous and frightened for their loved one. Brady worked his magic and did a few spins, sits and downs, weaves through my legs, and not taking treats resting on his nose. Then he proceeded to go from person to person for a pat or a hug, but the last person didn't want any part of him. "No, no," the man kept saying.

But Brady, looking deep into the man's eyes, inched himself a little closer, a little closer, a little bit more until he was right in the man's face. Brady didn't move, nor did the man. All of a sudden, we could see the man's face changing as he put his hand on top of Brady's head and said, "He's okay, he's okay!" Turns out he was forty-five years old and had never touched a dog. No wonder he was frightened! My Brady had made another room full of new friends. Then I heard him say, "He didn't have a chance. I knew I'd win him over, too." I stood there with my mouth open. I could actually hear my dog's thoughts!

No matter who we met, they were more relaxed and smiling after a visit with Brady. He also went with me to the bank, where the tellers and managers greeted us as old friends. While I was conducting my business with the tellers, Brady would greet the other customers waiting in line. Ninety-nine percent of the time, he got pats, hugs, tears in his fur, and lipstick on his forehead.

Our bank's logo was a bear. One time they did a promotion by giving away little stuffed teddy bears and of course, they gave a teddy bear to Brady. How did they know he liked stuffed animals? Because many times he would walk into the bank with a stuffed animal in his mouth, hoping someone would play tug-of-war with him. I took a picture of Brady that night, sleeping with his paws around that teddy bear, and sent it to the bank. The next time we went in, the manager told me that she had copied the photo onto the inner-office memo sheets for their meeting that week.

That Nose Again!

Brady's nose often got him into trouble. I was walking on the beach one beautiful morning with my trusted companion by my side, when suddenly his nose twitched. I knew that he had picked up a scent, but what was it? Brady ran down the beach, with me chasing after him, but he found the scent first. A smelly dead seal! As he was rubbing himself all over the seal, I heard, "What a great find!" I knew that was definitely Brady's thought—not mine—and it confirmed my suspicion that he and I were communicating through thought. As the years passed, I heard more and more of his thoughts.

As I retrieved my dog on the beach that morning, my eyes watered and I held my nose. Heading to our car, we encountered other people walking with their dogs, and I warned them about what was ahead. They politely thanked me, but the truth was that they already knew. They could smell me and Brady coming down the beach.

Brady and I would often go to Elings Park, where there was an off-leash area for dogs. One day, as we walked around the park on our way back to the car, up went the nose. Brady had picked up another scent, way on top of a hill. He galloped up that hill like a goat, with me in hot pursuit. I was trying to remember the commands I had learned in dog obedience school. *Here! Come! Stop! Wait!...* Oh, damn! Brady just looked at me, wagging his tail and saying, "I can't help it. It's a dog thing." As he came back down the hill with a guilty look on his face, I said, "I know, Brady.

It's a dog thing. The nose made you do it." He looked at me in a strange way and I heard, "It's about time you really heard me."

Being a retriever, Brady liked to retrieve. He knew where every avocado tree was in the neighborhood, and if he saw an avocado on the ground, he had to bring it home. There was a tennis court near us, and if he saw a tennis ball, he had to retrieve it too. One day when we got to the courts, there must have been a dozen tennis balls. Brady was beside himself with excitement! He ran around not knowing which ball to pick up first.

Have you seen the greeting card that has a golden retriever with three tennis balls in his mouth? Well, that's not my Brady. As much as he tried, he could fit only one ball in his mouth. And try he did, over and over. I heard, "This can't be happening, there has to be a way! Please let my mouth open wider." Then he turned to me with a resigned look on his face. It just couldn't be done. So I picked up two tennis balls, he took one in his mouth, and home we went. All the way home, Brady kept trying to get my two tennis balls into his mouth. When we got home, he corralled all three balls with his front paws, as happy as though he had just won a trophy.

After finishing a wonderful Thanksgiving Day turkey dinner, we cleared the dishes, loaded up the dishwasher, and took out the trash. Sitting around the table, we had decided to have a Jägermeister to settle our full tummies, when suddenly I heard a commotion coming from the side of the house. *Oh no*, I thought. *Where is Brady?* He had knocked over the garbage can and was filling his tummy with the leftovers—turkey bones, which can be deadly for dogs!

Into the car we hurried, with Gary driving and me crying, on our way to the doggie emergency room. The doc saw us right away. He said it had been a quiet night until we showed up. X-rays, an abdominal exam, and six hundred dollars later, we were sent home with instructions to give Brady soft bread soaked in mineral oil.

The X-rays showed that he had ingested small bones that would pass naturally the next day but no large bones that could splinter and puncture his intestines. That nose again.

As you know, cats cover up their business with dirt. Brady's nose, however, could always find the cats' business. He and I could be upstairs taking a nap, when up would go his nose. He would tear down the stairs and out the back door, and be eating it before I could even get down the stairs. Samantha would just look at him, probably thinking he was crazy and disgusting. How he could smell it from that far away remains a mystery. Any time we returned from going somewhere in the car, Brady would immediately run to the backyard to see if Samantha had left him a present. Luckily, as he got older this craving ceased. I guess what they say is true. As you get older, you develop a more sophisticated palate. That nose again. Another mystery of the dog world, I guess.

Brady's daily job was to go out front and pick up the newspaper. When I was training him for this chore, he always received a treat when he came back. In fact, he loved his job so much that after he got our paper, he would proceed down the street and pick up our neighbors' papers too. One morning, however, he didn't come right back. I went outside and looked down the street, but no Brady. Where did he go? Aha! Two houses down I saw that the garage door was open.

Brady was a friendly golden, so when he saw an open house or garage door, he thought it was an open invitation to come in. Sure enough, as I stepped into my neighbor's garage, I could see that the door to the house was also open. And as I moved farther into the garage, I heard Brady in the kitchen munching on dry cat food. I didn't know where the owners were, so I tiptoed in, got my dog, and beat a hasty retreat. Years later when I got to know those neighbors better, I told them about our visit. The wife had wondered how their cat had managed to eat—so quickly—all the food that she had just put out. We had a good laugh about it, and we're still friends today. That nose again.

The Neighborhood Gang

Brady had many friends in the neighborhood, animal and human alike. A golden retriever named Rusty lived down the street. Brady and I loved to walk in the rain, as did Rusty and her owners. We became good friends and took care of each other's dogs when either of us went away. They had a pool that Brady and Rusty loved to swim in. Rusty was fast and always got to the ball in the pool first, but then Brady got smart. He would pretend to go in the water, but actually he'd stop at the second step and wait there until Rusty came out of the pool with the ball in her mouth. As soon as she dropped it, he'd pick it up and run, with Rusty in pursuit. When Rusty had a litter of goldens, they kept one puppy and named her Daisy. She had no fear of anything and could do the best cannonball off the side of the pool that I ever saw.

Sam, a Bouvier des Flandres, lived down the street with Evie. He looked like a big black bear walking on a leash. Sam didn't really like most other dogs, but for some reason he liked Brady. Evie and I and our two dogs took many walks together, talking and sharing our day. Brady and Sam would walk together as if they were old souls reconnected. Sam really didn't like skateboards or cats, so he was always on the lookout for them. And just in case Sam found a cat or skateboard, Evie was always on the lookout for a lamppost to hang on to. Evie was from New York, as were we, so we often talked about that connection and shared jokes that only a New Yorker would understand. We still walk together today—only without our boys—and reminisce about the friendship that Brady and Sam shared, as we miss them terribly.

People who know me know of my love for animals. I was always taking care of dogs or cats, and finding lost dogs and trying to get them home. We've kept many strange dogs in our backyard as we waited for their owners to pick them up. We would just find dogs running around without their owners, so Brady would invite them home with us. In fact, we found the same two dogs twice, and twice had to call their owners to come and get them.

I took care of—and fell in love with—my next-door neighbors' four cats when their owners were away. Lucy and Vinnie were rag dolls, plus there was a beauty named Coco and a tabby named Motor. They were all indoor cats, although Motor wanted to go outside every morning.

On one dark, rainy day, Gary left early for work. Samantha and Brady were still asleep in their beds, and I was curled up waiting for the alarm clock to signal 7:00 a.m. Actually Brady was my alarm clock somehow always knowing when it was 7:00 a.m. and 4:00 p.m., because that meant it was time for a walk. That morning, Samantha's purr sounded strange as she walked over me, but when I looked in her bed, she was still asleep. So what was in bed with me? As I sat up, I saw that Motor was making himself at home. I guess his owners hadn't been able to find him before they had to leave for work. Since it was raining, he had come into our house through the cat door in our garage. Smart cat! Brady and Samantha didn't move, as if it was normal that Motor was in our house too.

That's what started our special relationship with Motor the Cat, who came and went as he pleased. Sometimes he stayed a short time, and sometimes all day. I can't tell you how many times Don or Shari, his owners, would call or come over and ask, "Is Motor with you?" And sure enough, he was asleep someplace nice and warm, taking his sweet time to be found.

When my parents visited us from New York, Motor would come over, make himself at home, and have breakfast with my dad. He would jump up on the outdoor picnic table where Dad was having cereal. Since Dad was used to having all my mom's creatures around, he gave Motor the milk left over from his cereal. Sometimes Motor got impatient with Dad for not finishing his cereal quickly enough, so he would just dip his paw into Dad's bowl and help himself to a paw of milk. Dad didn't mind, and they had breakfast together every morning. I'm not sure who enjoyed it more, Dad or Motor.

The Tooth, the Tooth, and Nothing but the Tooth

In addition to our hospital visits, Brady and I also went to grammar schools to talk to children about pet therapy work. Some children had been visited by a dog when they were in a hospital, and some had parents who were doctors or nurses and knew about therapy dogs. But some of the children didn't have any experience with dogs at all. So when Brady and I went in the classrooms, there were always lots of questions. First we did our tricks—sit, stay, spin, treat on the nose, ring the dinner bell, the usual entertainment. When we finished, we both took a bow and proceeded to meet and greet our audience. The children would share stories of their pets as we moved from one child to another.

Much of their fascination concerned Brady's teeth. Some children even pried open his lips to have a closer look. Brady just stood there and took it all. I heard, "I don't understand the interest, but okay." Sometimes they even touched his two fangs and wanted to know why they were so big. "Why don't we have fangs?" they would ask. In one class, a jokester told his fellow classmates that people don't have fangs because we aren't vampires. You can imagine the questions that immediately arose, so the teacher changed the subject to brushing one's teeth.

I whipped out Brady's toothbrush and explained that even dogs must to take care of their teeth. But they can't brush their own teeth, so we do it for them. Then I proceeded to brush Brady's teeth, explaining that we had special dog toothpaste. I also warned the students *not* to try brushing their own dogs' teeth at home. When we were finished, I heard a sigh from Brady with the thought, "We done yet?" Someone took photos of the children with Brady, and a week later he received a package of thank-you letters and drawings from the children of our visit.

Brady and I also worked with United Cerebral Palsy (UCP), visiting patients and children with special needs. This was a challenge for Brady, because they could not interact with a dog as other people did. Occasionally someone would hit him or pull on his leash, which confused Brady, but he took it all. I was right there to control the situation, and such actions were never intentional or harmful to Brady. Those people just lacked the motor skills necessary to control their movements, and Brady seemed to understand.

Once we visited a little six-year-old girl who had CP, and she became fixated on Brady. She followed him around the room, touched his teeth, looked in his ears and nose, and wanted to hold his leash and never let go. Another time, Gary and I volunteered to clean apartments at an independent-living facility for adults with CP in Carpenteria, and of course Brady came along. We ordered pizza for lunch, and everyone wanted to sit with Brady. I had packed his lunch, which consisted of two milk bones and doggie ice cream for dessert.

When we visited a classroom of deaf children, I had an interpreter but Brady was on his own. After our usual tricks, we took questions from the audience as Brady went to each child so they could pet him. He charmed the children, who were just precious. Some kids even asked if Brady could go home with them. Again, he seemed to understand that these children needed some extra TLC, and he was happy to provide it. They, too, were fascinated with his teeth. I heard him say, "What gives?" "I don't know," I whispered back, "but thanks for your patience." In the car on the way home, I heard, "Another good day." Then, with a sigh, Brady curled up in the back seat and rested his head on his front paws.

It's Too Soon

When I went downstairs on a Sunday morning, Brady was in the foyer and didn't want to get up. He hadn't eaten much of his dinner the previous evening, which was odd because he always had a good appetite, and then he hadn't gone upstairs to bed. His eyes looked different, and I could tell he wasn't feeling well. I tried to coax him upstairs, but he wouldn't go even for his special cookie. I knew something was wrong, and I told Gary I'd have to take him to the animal hospital the next morning. Sunday night, I slept on the floor with him, thankful when morning came so that I could call the veterinarian. They said to bring him right in.

That was Monday, March 21, 2011. The veterinarian said she thought it was pancreatitis and that Brady had to stay in the hospital for an IV drip and tests to confirm the diagnosis. During the exam, she found that Brady's liver was enlarged as well, so she recommended an ultrasound. The technician who did ultrasounds would be there on Wednesday. In the meantime, I was in touch with our regular veterinarian, who would supervise the test and call me with the results.

I was able to take Brady home that night, but he still didn't want to eat. I cooked him chicken and rice, but he ate only a handful. I slept with him again on Monday night, and on Tuesday morning I took him back at the hospital for more fluids. The house was so empty without him that I could hardly wait to pick him up that afternoon.

On Wednesday, March 23, I took Brady back to the hospital that morning for more fluids and the ultrasound. As I returned home, I had an uneasy feeling that something was really wrong with our boy. I was restless and spent the day pacing back and forth, until the phone call came... Two large tumors on his liver, bleeding in his spleen, kidneys not fully functioning, and confirmed pancreatitis. I was absolutely devastated. Not our boy! Brady was still a relatively young dog, at ten years old with his eleventh birthday coming up in May. This was happening too soon. The tears came and I couldn't stop them. I could barely tell Gary over the phone.

Picking Brady up that night, I still couldn't believe he was so sick. I knew the tumors might be cancerous, since Brady was a two-year survivor of a previous cancer occurrence. We had the option of going to a large animal hospital in Ventura for exploratory surgery to confirm the cancer. But if it was cancer, they wouldn't do anything because of where the tumors were located, plus then he would have to suffer with a large incision for the time he had left. His prognosis was not good, his organs were slowly shutting down, and it was just a matter of time. It could be several months or only a week—we just couldn't know how long.

Gary and I were in shock and didn't want to accept this. After talking more with the veterinarian, however, we decided to take Brady home and just love him, spend time with him, and visit our favorite places together for as long as we could. Since Brady's organs were failing, putting him through surgery might have postponed the inevitable for a few months, but we needed to think about what was best for him. We couldn't have stood it if Brady's last days were spent in pain and confusion. With the IV drips he had received at the hospital and a special diet, the pain from the pancreatitis seemed to be under control. He appeared to be comfortable and didn't seem to be in any pain from his other ailments.

That night he did eat, although not with gusto. But it was enough to give us a false sense of hope that maybe there had been a mistake, that things were not really so bad. That night, however, as we spent more time with Brady, reality set in. I slept with him again, talking to my boy and crying into his fur. I kissed his forehead and said, "You are the best puppy, and I love you so much. You helped so many people throughout your life—comforting them, listening to their secrets, and letting them cry into your fur. You always knew who needed your attention the most. You would look directly into their eyes as you understood their pain, and then eagerly lean against them and give them your unconditional love. You wanted to meet everyone, and everyone wanted to meet you. You are and always will be loved by so many people. Now it's time for me to take care of you and comfort you. I promise you will not be alone. I'll be with you always."

I told Brady that he was very sick and it would be time to say goodbye soon. I also promised him that Gary and I would not let him suffer pain just so we could keep him with us a little longer. As I let go of Brady, he looked so deeply and intensely into my eyes—his soul into my soul—that I knew he understood me.

We went for walks on the beach, because Brady loved the smells. We continued to take short walks every day to give Brady a chance to smell the "neighborhood news," and he went with us to our favorite places for lunch. We called some special friends whom he loved, so we could tell them what was going on. When they came to visit, he was still excited to see every one of them. He loved to ride in my little blue convertible with his ears in the wind, so we went for a ride every day. We were blessed to have a few extra days to love him, talk to him, and just have him with us.

One afternoon we were sitting together on the chaise longue on our patio, as we often did, and I asked Brady to tell me when it was time. "Give me a sign or send me your thought, so that I'll know," I told him. That night he didn't want to eat. His appetite never had returned to normal, but he had been eating a little. But that night was different. I slept with him on the floor again as I had every night since his diagnosis, but it was taking a long time for me to get to sleep. I finally drifted off from sheer exhaustion.

The day was March 31, 2011. At six o'clock that morning, just as daylight was breaking, I woke up and saw that he was already awake. With his head resting on his front paws, he was just looking at me. "It's time." I asked him if I had heard right. Was it time? He lifted his head, looked directly into my eyes, slowly closed his eyes for a moment, and then opened them again. I knew it was time to let him go.

Later that morning, we went on our last walk, and I could tell that he was uncomfortable. Pain was setting in as his organs gradually shut down. I phoned the veterinarian, who arrived at our house within the hour. Brady told me that his body was sick, he was tired, and he had to go. As with all our animals over the years, the decision to let go was devastating.

I have never had another companion like Brady, and the deep connection we shared will stay with me for the rest of my life. The last kiss on his forehead and the last tear in his fur were mine. Our sweet Brady boy went to sleep where he lived, at home and with dignity. He died in my arms, while I was wrapped in Gary's arms.

The tears came and were uncontrollable. Gary and I have never cried so hard in our lives. Even the veterinarian and the technician cried because they loved him too. Our last gift of love to our boy was to let him go. We knew it was the right thing to do.

Spirits?

On the afternoon of Brady's death, Gary and I were so incredibly sad. We could hardly believe he was gone. As we sat in silence on a bench in our backyard, I looked up and saw a beautiful monarch butterfly directly above us as it flew toward the front of the house. A minute later it came back, this time flying right in front of us. I could feel a whisper of a breeze from its wings brushing against my cheek, as a thought came through: "I'm okay." It was Brady sending us a message! I had heard that butterflies can carry the spirits of loved ones, especially if there has been a strong connection of love. Brady's spirit and mine—yes, we were connected in a special way. Gary believed it, too.

I spent the rest of the afternoon just walking around, numb and missing Brady so much. Seeing his toys, bowl, and leash, I had to get out of the house, so I went outside and sat on our patio. Knowing we had done the right thing didn't make this any easier. I looked up and there was the monarch again, only this time it stopped and fluttered right in front of my face. Then I heard, "Don't be sad, Mommy." Brady's thought came through again, telling me he was still there with me.

It seems like only yesterday, but it has been five years since Brady passed away. As I sit here writing, the tears are streaming down my face again, and I can barely see the keyboard. My life with my boy, my partner—all the adventures and mischief, the hospitals and schools, and the many lives he touched. The connection we shared was a once-in-a-lifetime experience that many people never have. It was a pleasure and privilege to share Brady's gentle spirit with so many people. So many more memories are flooding back, it's like it was yesterday. I celebrate that gentle spirit who touched many lives, especially mine. I believe in destiny, and I believe the way Brady came into my life was meant to be. He chose me to help him fulfill his purpose on earth.

That monarch butterfly visited many times. Sometimes he had a message, but not always. I still see the monarch in strange places, and I believe it is Brady letting me know he is still here. Sometimes thoughts will pop into my head and I know it's him. I believe spirits can go anywhere and aren't limited by time and place. I was in the backyard last year just looking at the beautiful clouds when two hummingbirds flew past me so close, I thought they were going to hit me. As they came back around, chasing each other, I actually felt a breeze from their wings. I knew it was Brady. The thought that came through was "This is so much fun." And the birds did look like they were having fun, flying at lightning speed all around the yard and making me smile. Whether that is Brady's spirit or not, I guess I'll never really know. But that's what I believe as I remember our special connection.

When Brady passed away, my soul was so sad. I had to find a way to celebrate his life rather than dwell on his death. I started writing down my thoughts, and eventually *Lipstick on His Forehead and Tears in His Fur: Adventures of a Therapy Dog* was published as a tribute to Brady and all he did. The next year I wrote *Charlie-B: The Therapy Dog*, a children's version with illustrations of a special puppy. In *Charlie-B*, I wrote about how Brady came into my life, and I explain the life lessons that puppies have to learn, just like children. I was told by someone who believes in the spirit world that Brady would help me write our story. I believe he did so, and he is still right by my side today. I know that this connection we share is so deep that it continues, even after death. Brady had a great sense of humor, and I like to believe he is smiling with me as I write this book. Were our spirits soul mates? You decide for yourself, but I already know my answer.

We lost our Samantha two years ago. Letting her go was another hard decision for us, but it was the right one for her. I think Samantha also came to visit me about a month after she passed. When she was still alive, Samantha would come and sit with me every afternoon on the patio couch as I read the paper. When she started getting older, she would just watch the birds and lizards as they appeared in our yard. Sometimes she would utter a chirping noise to let me know she saw the critters but she didn't chase them anymore.

It was a beautiful, warm, sunny day as I came out of the house to sit on the couch on our patio. There on the couch, in the same spot where Samantha used to lie, was a lizard just looking at me as if it had been waiting for me. I carefully sat down across from it. It stayed a while and then scurried up to the top of the couch near my shoulder. This might seem creepy, but for some reason it wasn't to me. I looked at that lizard and said, "Samantha, couldn't you have come back as something a little more warm and fuzzy? A lizard, really?" I have no idea why I said this; it just came out. The lizard started to move its head up and down like they do, almost as if telling me it understood. After a few minutes it scurried away.

The next afternoon, that lizard was back on the couch. We've always had lizards in our yard, although none had ever gotten on the furniture. But there it was again, just looking at me. On the third afternoon, the couch was unoccupied. But when I sat down to read the paper, the lizard showed up again and joined me on the couch. The creature moved so fast that it scared me. As I jumped up, I said, "Samantha, this is not cute anymore." The lizards have all stayed on the ground since then. It makes me wonder, though.

Brooklyn and Kitty-Kitty

Our life is quiet now. We enjoy spending time with our children and granddaughter every chance we get. Gary is still running marathons; in fact, he's run well over seventy by now. I'm partially retired, which gives us more time to travel and visit our children and families and for me to write about all the critters who have been part of my life over the years.

I have had a therapist for about four years now. She comes to the house a few times a week, or sometimes I pick her up. She's a very good listener, never interrupting my thoughts. Sometimes we go for long walks where I can cry, complain, reminisce about Brady or just talk out loud. My therapist never judges me. I can sing out loud with or without my radio, and sometimes she even sings with me. I can talk about any subject, even politics or religion, and she never disagrees or argues with me.

The only problem is, she sheds. Brooklyn, my therapist, is a golden retriever, husky mixed dog rescued from Bakersfield. Her family lives next door to us. I started walking her when her daddy was at work and when they had their first baby. When her family travels, Brooklyn stays with us. We take her to a restaurant or the beach, and she seems very content to be with us.

One afternoon I fried some bacon to use in a recipe to take to a party. I was draining the bacon on a paper towel, which I had pushed up against the window so Brooklyn wouldn't get it. At one point I turned to the refrigerator to get the rest of the ingredients out, which took maybe five seconds. With my hands full, I then turned back toward the counter, where I saw... the paper towel on the ground, the bacon gone, and Brooklyn licking her lips! Gone. A pound of bacon, gone in seconds. Brooklyn had quietly reached up with her paws, done a little hop, and got hold of that bacon. I called my veterinarian and explained what had happened, but she said not to worry. The cooked bacon would pass right through her, although it would have been worse if the bacon had been raw. That dog was just so fast!

Another time when Brooklyn was at our house, I was cooking hamburger sliders for dinner. I made the patties, put them on a paper plate, and then set the plate on top of the toaster oven. Remembering how Brooklyn got to the bacon the last time, I figured there was no way she could get to those patties on top of the toaster oven. While I was putting plastic wrap around them, the phone rang. It was Gary, calling to tell me that he was going to be a little late coming home. That phone call lasted maybe ten seconds. I turned back to the counter, and sure enough, Brooklyn had stretched up far enough to get her paw on the edge of the paper plate and knock it to the floor. She was just starting to eat patty number two! "Drop it!" I screamed. She stopped chewing, but she didn't spit it out. So I pried that dog's jaw open and pulled the patty out—not a pleasant experience. Brooklyn is just so fast.

Again, I called my veterinarian and explained what had happened. She said Brooklyn would be fine since she hadn't eaten a lot of the raw meat. However, she told me to give the dog some Pepto Bismol to settle her stomach. Well, that worked really well. I filled an eyedropper with Pepto and then squirted it into Brooklyn's mouth. The problem was that she didn't swallow it. Instead, she spit it out, shaking her head and splattering pink Pepto all over the kitchen floor, cabinets, door, and me. Ugh! Luckily it didn't stain or I'd have a pink kitchen.

Since we have animals, we are always very careful about what we leave in our backyard. But one time Brooklyn found an old box of fertilizer and decided to explore. Once again, I phoned my veterinarian. As soon as I said, "This is Doris," she responded with, "Let me guess. Brooklyn?" I proceeded to explain what had happened, and this time the veterinarian wanted to see both the dog and the box. The box was filled with organic fertilizer, which would probably pass through the dog if she had eaten any of it. Nevertheless, the veterinarian examined Brooklyn and pumped her stomach, just to be sure.

Since then, when Brooklyn is here and I need to cook something, I put any food inside the cabinet. Her owners told me she has taken cupcakes, biscuits, and other food off the children's plates when no one was watching. So the bottom line is that Brooklyn is a crafty, clever thief.

Brooklyn spends the day with me when her owners are at work. One afternoon she was intrigued with one of the rocks in our garden. I thought she had cornered a lizard, as she often does, but then I saw what looked like flies buzzing around her. As I came closer, I realized they were bees. Brooklyn had found a hive. I took her home so she wouldn't get into the hive and get stung.

When Gary arrived home, I told him about the hive. He went to investigate because we couldn't see an actual hive. As he took a stick and poked behind the rock, I told him that might not be a good... I didn't even get to say the word *idea*, because Gary started screaming and running around. There must have been thirty or more bees chasing him! I grabbed the water hose and started spraying him and the bees, hoping they would stop stinging him so I could get him inside. The bees finally left, but not before stinging Gary many, many times. They stung him through his shirt and socks, as well as his legs and up his shorts to his thighs.

We had heard that making a paste of meat tenderizer would ease the pain, but the stings were so painful that I went to the pharmacy for some lotion. The only thing that helped a little was ice, but still, Gary didn't sleep all night because of the pain. I called Hydrex Pest Control the next morning, and a guy showed up within the hour in a full white bee suit complete with helmet. As he was looking at the rock, I asked if he could see the bees. "Yes, and this is war," he said. They weren't bees—they were yellow jackets, which make their nests in the ground and can be very aggressive. He also said Gary was lucky that they had flown away, because often they will just keep attacking and attacking. Lesson 101: Don't poke at things, ever!

Brooklyn is a very smart dog and she loves her family, especially her daddy. I think she knows he saved her. Sometimes Brooklyn would be curled up on my foyer floor, very content, when all of a sudden she would start whining. She'd find me and lead me to the front door, obviously wanting to go out in the worst way. When I opened the front door, she would bolt for her house. She knew the sound of her family's car, and she had heard it coming down the street. Before they could even park and get out of the car, she was there to welcome them home. Amazing! They are a lucky family to have such a great dog, and Brooklyn is lucky to have such a wonderful family.

Over the past year, a cat has been coming to visit us. She wandered into our back yard one night and kept coming back. I've seen her around our neighborhood and the local school, but for some reason she has decided that our house is her house. She has adopted us, and we have come to love her. She comes and goes as she pleases, though now she come home at dusk and is very content to spend the night with us. She especially likes to sleep with us under the covers and have her face rubbed. She plays on the stairs, doing somersaults and all the funny antics that cats do. I don't know her name, so I call her Kitty-Kitty and she comes running. She rubs her head on us to mark us as her own, and sometimes brings us lizards and birds as gifts. Thanks to Kitty-Kitty, we once again have the adventure of trying to capture birds flying around in our house and lizards scurrying around the floor.

One day Kitty-Kitty brought in a baby bunny. She carried the bunny all the way upstairs, where I was writing, without putting so much as a scratch on it. When she dropped it at my feet, looking very proud of herself, the bunny hopped into my closet. I called for Gary to help, but neither of us could find that little one. When we did spot it, the bunny would quickly hop away behind the desk, or bed, or dresser. Every time we got close, it hopped away. So Gary went to get the cat carrier from the garage. Our idea was to corner the bunny in the closet, let Kitty-Kitty into the closet, and have her chase bunny into the carrier. Well, the only thing that jumped into the carrier was Kitty-Kitty. That little bunny jumped over Kitty-Kitty and escaped again.

Gary and I just sat on the floor and laughed. As we looked around our little bedroom, the bed was pulled out from the wall, the pillows were on the floor, shoes and luggage had been hauled out of the closet, the desk was shoved into the middle of the room, and the pages of this book were scattered all over. It looked as though there had been an earthquake! And after all this, we still didn't have the bunny.

Finally I got some garden gloves and a flashlight, and I bravely ventured into the closet. Right there, in the far corner and up against the wall, was the cute little guy. Exhausted from the hunt, he let me grab him and put him into the cat carrier. Gary then took the bunny down the street to the creek where other bunnies lived. Boy, did that little furry guy have a story to tell his bunny friends that night!

My hope is that you have enjoyed my journey with all the critters in my life. Think of yours and celebrate them too. When all is said and done, our animals just want to be with us—to protect us, share our lives, make us laugh, and yes, when it's time to say goodbye, our hearts break. But our journey with them is worth everything as their paws remain on our hearts forever.

And I smile.

Oh, what a ride it's been.

About the Author

Even in her early years in Germany, DJ Clancy always had animals in her life. Her love for animals is apparent in all three of her books. When her beloved golden retriever, Brady, passed away, she felt the need to share their story by celebrating his life rather than mourning his death. Brady was a certified therapy pet who had the unique gift of knowing who needed his unconditional love. *Lipstick on His Forehead and Tears in His Fur: Adventures of a Therapy Dog* recounts the amazing connection between Ms. Clancy and Brady and the wonderful work they did together.

Ms. Clancy's second book, *Charlie-B*, is based on her first book, but the story is adapted for children. Well illustrated in bright colors and filled with easily understood rhymes, *Charlie-B* is an early reader with a life lesson in each paragraph. It's a story about the joy of getting a puppy and teaching him about people and the world, just as you would teach a child. Memories of your own childhood puppy will surface as you read *Charlie-B*.

Ms. Clancy's ability to see humor in her animals shines through once again in this book, *My Furry, Four-Footed Friends: And Other Creatures Great and Small.* Concentrating on her cats and dogs, she cites their differences and similarities in the way they pursue and achieve similar goals. You will smile, laugh, cry, and smile again as she takes you through her life. This is a delightful read for anyone who loves animals. The Q and A with her dog and cat is not to be missed!

DJ Clancy lives in Santa Barbara, California, with her husband.

Visit her at www.djclancy.com

Printed in the United States
By Bookmasters